Rhymes
our Tin

Rhymes for our Times

by Fran

THE CHOIR PRESS

First published in the United Kingdom in 2019 by
The Choir Press

ISBN 978-1-78963-111-1

Acknowledgments

Illustrations by Amy Bright
www.facebook.com/nelliebee
nelliebeeuk@yahoo.com

Project management by Judy Sharp

www.isitjustme.uk
judysharp@isitjustme.uk

To my late husband, Guy

Contents

THE OLDEN DAYS

I remember when, in days of yore,
dustmen came to your own back door.
With a smile and a cheery wave
took everything you couldn't save.
Paper, eggshells, all went in –
you only had the one dustbin.
Now, however, things have changed:
'Hygiene Operatives' they're named.
All must possess, to high degree,
knowledge of the chemistry
of all the objects they collect,
for our environment to protect.
I cannot see with my old eyes
of what these wrappers do comprise:
is it paper, or is it plastic?
To know all this would be fantastic!
Where should I put this glass? This tin?
Must throw them in the proper bin.

It really isn't fair you know
for me to be bewildered so.
I'll put out my son's old bicycle–
they can't pretend *that's* not recyclable!
They did – I'm fined, again –
that's fifty quid gone down the drain.
time I'll opt to go to jail
where all my waste goes in a pail!

A HOLIDAY

It's 20 years since we went away
together on a holiday, so
I've been researching on the net
something we will never forget.
In the Arctic they have built
a hotel that is up on stilts.
A nice double room, they say,
is only £5,000 a day,
all meal pills included.
There's a fine programme of sightseeing provided
All the places I've long decided,
We'd love to see, explore –
the moon, Mars, Venus and more
that I've never even heard of!
You wear these special goggles, you see,
much better than the old 3D,
and you sit in a theatre while all around
the magic of the planets abound
with creatures and sights that could never be found
on boring old Earth!
Think about it!

I asked again the very next day.
Here's what my dearest had to say:
"I know that I'm a bit of a stick-in-the-mud
but I've been having a think down the pub.
This trip of yours could startle and frighten –
why can't we just go back to Brighton?"

SUMMER FARE

I sit here eating strawberries and cream
grown by my neighbour in her patch of green,
and look out of the window at my little plot.
I'd hoped to see some summer fare
luscious and fruiting, ready there.
My neighbour's son had offered, you see,
to tend my garden and share with me
the results of his labours.
He really is a nice young bloke –
but rows and rows of weed to smoke?
Ought I to go and tell his mum?
'Cos what he needs is a good smacked bum!

JANE'S TRIP

Hello God, my name is Jane,
didn't expect to be here again
so soon.
We planned together, didn't we?
But I cut it short, at 23.
My lovely parents did all they could,
I grew up in a neighourhood
that gave me such a wonderful start.
School was fun, encouraged my art;
plenty of friends, plenty of fun.
But then I found a way to go
and enhance my life – just throw
these pills down and see what happens!
Wow! What a kaleidoscope of patterns!
This was addictive, I couldn't stop,
I needed more to go over the top.
So here I am, God, as you see –
and I was only 23.

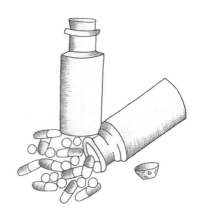

ELEVENSES

When I wake up I sometimes say,
"There's nothing much to do today."
I've got to make a decision.
To go down to town and have a read
or buy some things I really don't need.
Change that jumper you bought in Marks:
you're much too old for lurex and sparks!

Along the High Street I vaguely roam –
now there's a shop like second home
to me.
Why on earth must you persist
in doing something you should resist?
There's a table inside, not too bad today.
I know the staff well, I hear them mutter
"Look out, here comes that pink-haired nutter!
Flat white, croissant, jam and butter,
that's all she ever has, while all around
There's cakes galore!"
But who are the gluten-free, sugar-free
flour-less, fat-less cakes for?
There's nothing in there that fattening
could be:
I'm very strong willed, so not for me.
I carry my tray and I look for a table
with a soft chair if I am able
to find one in the window.

Five minutes later, guilt sets in
I see all these ladies going to the gym
next door.
What an assortment of gear they wear –
I thought I was brave having pink hair!
Avert your eyes, relax, have some fun,
read a free copy of The Sun.
After five minutes that's all done.
I'm a bit tired,
I feel my eyes begin to glaze.
I look around me through the haze.
At the end of the room there's a long
table
with six young mums as far as I am able
to make out.
They're surrounded by, as my eyes
unravel,
things designed for inter-space travel:
(they used to be called prams!)
Three small people rushing about
who cannot speak but only shout.

They're in Star Wars clothes and swords they're clashing:
even their little shoes are flashing –
(I do hope those swords are plastic.)
Oblivious to this the mums chat on and on
'til suddenly there's quite a loud PING
I think it means a text is coming in.
"Oh look," says one, "its dear little Oscar texting me".

"I think that's wrong," another one said,
"at under 6 months it'll mess with his head."
"I don't agree, I think it's neat –
at nine months old my daughter could tweet!"
You don't understand.
These are new rules:
If you want them to go
to very good schools:
"Well, may we see what the darling boy said
to prove it hasn't messed with his head?"
"Of course," said Mum, "I'm just so proud
of Oscar, I'll read it aloud:

"Go home at once you lazy cow
I need to be fed, I mean **right now!**
If you don't go now you know
what I'll do:
my soaking wet nappy will contain
a large poo
for you to clean."
"Ah how sweet," they explain with a nervous titter
"he'll soon be ready to go on Twitter!"
The voices fade.
A tap on the shoulder,
I hear a voice say,
"do you mind if I remove the tray?"
Oh dear.
My rational thinking drops to zero
when wasting hours in Caffè Nero.

I'M ONLY A BABY

I'm only a baby still you see
I'll have to use telepathy –
I remember that!
They cradle me in their arms
and flee from whatever it is that harms
people like us.
They stop to nourish me along the way –
what have they had to eat today?
So on and on and on they flee
then come to a place it sounds like the sea.
"You've got a choice" the rough voice said,
"if you stay here you'll all be dead,
soon."
"Just give me all the money you've got
we'll get you out of here but not
until this boat is full to the brim,
I just hope that all of you can swim."
They sit together, shoulder to shoulder,
but halfway out we hit a boulder.
We get tipped out, my parents and I,
I know it's time to say goodbye –
Where _could_ they have learned to swim?

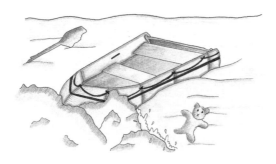

A NEST EGG

Down at the club for OAPs
they do their best to try and please,
persuading us all that we're really quite rational,
so I paid into the sweep for the coming Grand National.
(a daft thing to do – I never win anything).
One week later to my surprise
I got a call – "you've won a prize
on an each-way bet (what's that?)
£300!"
A nest egg indeed, I need to plan.
The savings pot is on the shelf
but if I leave it there I'll help myself
over the weeks for this and that
and waste it all on tut and tat.
No, I'll do the good and sensible thing,
go to the bank and pay it all in,
except for two fivers which I'll put in my pinny –
keep some to spend, you stupid ninny!
Now the bank only opens twice a week,
so I went on the bus next Thursday to seek
a safe haven for my nest egg.

"Why, Mrs B," said the clerk with a grin,
"not taking out, but paying in?
That's a change!"
"Now I have to ask – it's the law you see –
have you laundered this money? 'Cos that would be
A CRIME! AGAINST THE STATE!"
Unbidden the memory came to me
of my pinny's two fivers in the wash.
I can't go to prison, I'm much too posh!
They must have a gadget now it seems
that can see inside our washing machines!
Enraged I said, "Just give it me back,
I'm shocked you could even think of that!"
I went back home, still clutching my nest,
trying to work out what to do next.
Then I remembered what Mum always said:
"Put it under the mattress, your side of the bed,
it'll be quite safe there!"
And so it was –
'til I went and spent it!

A MODERN TOT

The babe arrived – oh what joy!
It was a darling little boy.
The parents smiled:
they saw at once
their child would never be a dunce.
So with an eye to future earning
they set about his early learning.
At three months old he went to school –
considered now "so very cool" –
and there he was exposed you see
to all the new technology.
At six months old his teachers said,
"there's something wrong inside his head.
He does not speak – alas! alack!"
They called the worried parents back.
All gathered round and then they heard
the little treasure's very first word.
What would he say, this modern tot?
Just: "www.DOT!"

PETE'S TEA

Why am I lying on this hill?
Everywhere's so quiet and still.
Where's the rest of my company?
My bloomin' hands have gone all numb,
I can't feel this bloody gun.
'Ere, perhaps I've caught a fourpenny one!
Hah, don't be daft you stupid git,
You would know if you'd been hit!
I'll just stay here, as Sarge would say,
ready to fight another day.
What's that light coming close to me?
It's so bright I can hardly see.
Gawd! There's me mum! She's long been gone.
Why is she looking so well and young?
She's stretching out her hand to me
"Now come on Pete, you can't stop here,
You'll catch your death of cold, my dear.
"Just you come with me, my lad –
Together we'll go and find your dad:
"We'll have us tea."
I'M HOME !

A RESCUE?

I sit in the café and look at the scene
nothing could be more calm and serene.
A beautiful village pond!
This one is special, it's obvious to me
Aerated daily, as clean as can be.
Two islands for ducks with plentiful greenery,
large houses with gardens complete the scenery.
A mother appears, with kids moving slow
walking behind her on a morning stroll.
They're heading for the bench I know
where little children are wont to throw their treats
over the fence while mothers gossip.
Then comes the sound of a slight kerfuffle –
four elegant ladies are trying to shuttle
our family home.

Mother responds with a furious "quack" –
"come on kids, we've got to get back:
they'll try and push us under the wire,
resulting in something rather dire."
The elegant ladies scurry behind
anxious now a solution to find
to the dilemma.
But mother duck says – "do not doubt
we'll just get in the way we got out!"
"Oh good," say the ladies with a sheepish titter,
"we'll put this rescue out on Twitter!"

Silver surfers, it seems to me,
have nothing at all to do with
the sea.
So instead of getting all cold
and wet,
they surf something called the
Internet –
that sounds interesting!
So I asked my son how
I could join:
"you can't Mum," he said, "it's only on line,
which means you have to get a COMPUTER!!"
"No, my dear, I simply will not,
do you think I've completely lost the plot?"
A dinosaur may be what I am
but lose my savings in a scam?
NO THANKS!"

PS: I wonder what skateboarders do?

LONELINESS

Loneliness takes many forms:
it hides itself within the norms
of rational thinking!
A loneliness that has no name
is quite impossible to explain.
I'm getting towards the end of my life
and realise that all the trouble and strife
was just what I had agreed to do –
I can't think why??
Several partners, two lovely sons –
why can't I accept life as it comes?
There's a loneliness you see
that's deep within the heart of me.
Nothing will make it go away
'til I reach home at the end of my day.

DOGGIEBIX

I don't know why, this particular day,
I didn't go home the usual way.
I knew that mum wouldn't want me to roam
down these side streets all alone –
so that's why I did it!
Then I felt around my feet
a little dog, he was really sweet.

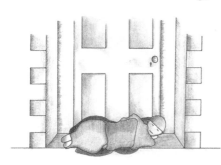

He gave a great big whine and so
I knew just where he wanted to go.
There's a bundle of rags in this
doorway here,
It's what he wants, he makes it clear.
He nudges the rags, a voice comes
out,
"Look 'ere lad, just go away,
I ain't got the strength to beg today,
you'll have to scrounge whatever you can."
I look around and there's a shop
(the sort where mum wouldn't let me stop)
so I'll go in!
I'm a bit afraid, but what a lark,
then a voice comes out of the dark:
"What can I do for you, my dear?"
"I've only got 50p," I say,
"I need to feed my dog today."
I look around, the name just sticks –
I'll buy a box of Doggiebix!

I give them some,
then run off home, I mustn't be late,
Can't tell my mum, (she's not a mate).
I'll hide them under my bed I think,
otherwise there'll be a stink!
It's Saturday the very next day
me and my friends go out to play.
When I get home I see at once
something's up!
"Now my girl, is this one of your tricks,
starting eating Doggiebix?"
"You must **not** eat these as special treats
they can't be eaten just like sweets!
And, while we're at it, under your bed
is like a dustbin!" That's what she said.
I had to tell her then, you see,
otherwise she'd keep on at me.
"Now I work at the Social, as you know
my dear
so together why don't we go and find
this man and his dog, you've been so kind,
perhaps he'll let us help him now."
We found him there in the same old place
but something had happened to his face.
(Not the dog – the man I mean),
and the dog was trying to lick it clean!

"Now come on, sir, this isn't right,
you can't stay here another night,"
Mum says.
"I'll make a call, I'll wait till they come
and take you somewhere clean and warm."
"I ain't going! I know my rights!"
My mother's face puts on that look
that means no nonsense will she brook:
I know it well!
"You're worried about your dog, I know –
what will happen if you go?

My daughter and I have hatched a plan:
We'll take him with us, if you say we can.
Feed him up, let him play
in our garden every day."
(What? She never let me have a dog!)
"And when you're fit and well and bright,
and have a little place to live,
come and get him back again –
That's your right!"
"OK," said the voice from under the rags,
"I suppose he can lodge with you for a bit!"
The ambulance came and took him away,
He seemed more cheerful then, I'd say.

I picked up the dog (wrapped in a rag,
Mum said he needed the smell of his dad).
"He's full of fleas you can safely bet,
We'll have to take him to the vet.
We can't take him home scratching like that!
I know a vet, he owes me one!
We'll have to see what can be done."
"Oh," said the man, "I have to say
This poor little chap is in a bad way."
I shot up my hand, "please, I'll pay, I'll pay,
I've got to take him home today."
"You will," said the vet, "no need to pay,
This can be my good deed for the day."
So off we went, my mum and me,
Had lovely cup of tea.
Went to fetch him – what a sight!
De-loused, de-flead, all shiny and bright.
Bought a lead, let him run,
You could see he'd never had such fun.
Such a lovely end to a fix
And all because of Doggiebix!
PS – I love my mum, she's a mate!

IN PRAISE OF CHEESE

I search out the area called Delicatessen
When I feel in need of a geography lesson!
The counter is filled from left to right
with all kinds of cheeses
designed to delight
and challenge the tastebuds (but not mine).
It's the places of origin that challenge me,
to puzzle out where they could possibly be.

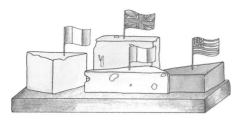

In Europe? Or Asia?
Or possibly Australia?
In geography I was always a
failure!
Now I'm a selective cheese lover
and cook
And will proudly boast of just
A strong English Cheddar
Melted on toast!

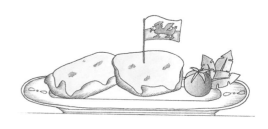

22

JUST FILL IN THIS FORM

I ring the Council and I'm told (I think
by a human voice) to get a form from the GPO.
OK, well I know where that is (or was)
so I'll go down there and have a go.
"Would you like some help to fill it in?"
the nice clerk asks.
"no thank you," I reply.
What a cheek – I've been filling in forms since he was a boy!
I sit down at home at my antique desk
to comply with the questions they request.
Name? Address? Date and place of birth?
House owner? Mother's maiden name?
Rate payer? Any convictions?
One letter per square please
and don't go over the lines!
Return the form. On line is best.
What's that? I'll just sneak down when the Council is closed
and post it under the mat.
Dear oh dear, my head's in a spin –
and all I want is another dustbin!

I KNOW WHAT I AM

"You're prisoner 543," he said,
"Just get in here and duck your head,
And if you take my good advice,
You'll keep it that way
And live to see another day.
There's blokes in here would beat you up
As soon as look at you, young pup."
I stare around my prison cell.
What brought me here I know quite well.
Have I escaped the gang from hell?
I joined when I was 13, see,
It was a great honour for little me.
We smoked our fags,
Or a few smash and grabs ...
We never hurt no-one as I could see,
We stole some beers, we robbed a till,

Then things became more violent still.
I just knew then the day would come
When someone would produce a gun.
I'd be involved in something more
Than I had ever bargained for.

We went to rob a hole in the wall,
That's all.
There was someone drawing a pile of cash out,
We all moved in to grab the lot.
Then there came a very loud shot.
"It was meant as a warning!" our leader said,
"I didn't intend to shoot him dead."
So now you know why I am here,
An accomplice to murder is what I am
I don't care what they do to me here.

25

AN OUTING

An Outing has always meant to me
a good excuse for a naughty cream tea.
A visit to a Stately Home or Castle
is always an obligatory part of the parcel.
My friend came round to me and said,
"why don't we go somewhere else instead –
it'll make a change!
I've seen a trip in this week's local –
just think about it before you get vocal.
It's a hundred miles awaybut could be a lark –
24 hours in a huge Primark!"
PS – I might go!

WISHFUL THINKING

Oh dear! Oh dear! My mind's a riot!
I really ought to find a diet.
What is this tyre around my tum
that's moving down towards my bum?
It can't be hard to find one that
eliminates this awful fat.
I'll Google one – that will work –
and from this task I will not shirk.
It must allow a smallish host
of tiny things I like the most –
(like choccy biks and maybe toast) –
that won't be hard. But hey!
Don't resolutions fade away
in the cold light of day?
I'll count on that, then, have a treat,
and then perhaps go back to sleep!

PURE LOVE

I looked up to see her standing there –
a lady pushing a large wheelchair.
"Do you mind if I leave her here in this seat
while I go and queue for something to eat?"
"Not at all," I said and, as I am able,
removed myself to an adjoining table.
With unlined face and eyes so blue,
she restlessly searched the growing queue
for a familiar face. Reassured,
she's got a soft toy she's waving about
though never a sound from her mouth comes out.
But I can't mistake the looks of glee
at all the goodies brought for her tea.

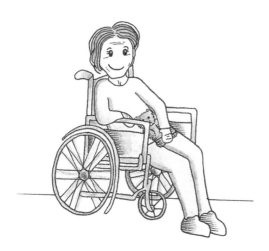

Mouthful by mouthful she's lovingly fed
with chocolate cake and nice tea bread.
A Wet Wipes produced to clear it away.
I get up to leave and smile and ask
"Wasn't that quite a fiddly task?"
"Yes but she's my daughter you see,
I bring her each year for her birthday tea."
"How old is she?" I struggle to say,
"Well, she's just 49 today."
I left, my heart humbled to the core –
I haven't seen pure love before.

AN ACHILLES' HEEL

My friend Gail who lives with me
is normally sensible as can be.
But there is one thing that I can reveal
shows to all her Achilles' heel.
A hairdresser by trade she will own
and so can never leave her hair alone!
It's up, it's down, it's green, it's brown –
or pink, or blue …
or some other wondrous hue!
But today she's gone and had a perm –
all curly and wild and like a child.
I rack my brains – who does she resemble?
Oh heck! A rather older Shirley Temple!
Soon she'll be singing – oh please make her stop –
"on the good ship Lollipop!

A VISIT WITH MUM

I enter the room with some apprehension,
but there's no sign of nervous tension.
I survey every person sitting there,
each in their own appointed chair.
I take a seat to sit by Mum,
who smiles at me in a sweet, vague way
that makes me wonder if this is the total sum
of what I'm going to have today. Of Mum.
But all may not be as it seems,
for many and varied are the dreams
of encounters, journeys and familiar scenes
they choose to remember and enjoy once more,
or sometimes new things they want to explore.
They wander, unfettered,
only attached by a gossamer thread
to the world they knew inside their head.
So do not despair as you hold their hands -
they pursue their lives in other lands
we cannot share.
How do I know this?
Because I've heard them.

A SIX O'CLOCK DILEMMA

When drinking gin and diet tonic
results for me are purely platonic.
There's nothing there my heart to vex,
thinking of long-forgotten sex ...
What it needs, oh how ironic,
is another gin – and full-fat tonic!

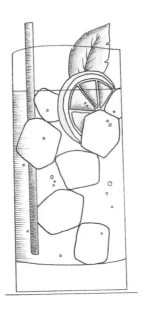